Gallery Books
Editor Peter Fallon

THE HIGH CAUL CAP

Medbh McGuckian

THE HIGH
CAUL CAP

Gallery Books

The High Caul Cap
is first published
simultaneously in paperback
and in a clothbound edition
on 30 October 2012.

The Gallery Press
Loughcrew
Oldcastle
County Meath
Ireland

www.gallerypress.com

ISBN 978 1 85235 543 2 *paperback*
     978 1 85235 544 9 *clothbound*

A CIP catalogue record for this book
is available from the British Library.

Contents

These Latinized Snows *page* 11
Research into Haloes 12
Woman Examining Her Breasts in a Mirror 13
The Nth of Marchember 14
The Museum of Touch 16
Cousin Alice 17
A Supplement to the Withering 18
Corner of Field with Farm 19
Broken Pot Used as Writing Material 20
Woman Kept in a Casket 21
Kaluza's Law 23
Maroon-backed Ledger 24
Her Everyday Comportment 25
The Seven Times Mother 26
She Wears the Sky 27
Goddess of the Candlelight during Childbirth 28
The Mirroring Mother 29
Why I Don't Get Down and Pray in the Sunroom 31
On Cutting One's Finger While Reaching for Jasmine 32
Willowware Cup 33
Sweet Dream Just Before Christmas 35
Sandpaper Letters 36
The Meaning of Margaret's Hands 38
Seated Woman 40
The Mercyseat 41
The Spirit of the Mother 42
The High Caul Cap 45
Sunburst in E Major 46
The Vine Forestlight 47
Rose Inhabited by a Bee 48
Master of the Female Half-lengths 49
The Doll Funeral 50
A Death Horoscope 51
Dormition: Madonna with Trees 52
Gold Star Mother 55
The Plumrose Anemone 57

Operation Spring Wind 58
The Honey Vision 59
Ascent to Perception Temple 60
The Wearing of Brooches 61
The Mules that Angels Ride 63
The Skull Nest 64
Dúlamán 65
Sung Death 66
The Ocean River 67
The Light Called Opalescence 68
Notebook of Sleeps 69
Sibyl with Guitar 70
M and a Half Street 71
Buttermilk Shade 72
Dark Lips, Jade Pillow 74
The Blood Trolley 75
Receiving Non-rebirth 77
The Flower of the Moment of What Comes Easily 79

*in memory of Siobhán
and Mary*

These Latinized Snows

This room should be read as a preface
to an experience which occurred
many miles before: light-of-day
simplicity in the administered space,
accepting the pre-set view,
though belts of country miles in width
have been swept away.
The electric fluid has taken to carrying
the mail, like a blood-opening heart buried under
a sundial, or the undiluted Nile.

By quietly slipping in the word 'eva' ('only'),
those who delicately thread the needles
lay a motionless finger on a forearm
to show through this so-called non-blue
otherwise sheltering the dance the woman
is about to break into, wearing her belatedness
like a far grander blanket.

Long after other fireplaces have subsided
two savage arcs are flaming like weeds
in snow from end to end of your lovely,
symbolic city where one day
marketgoers would again arrive by train . . .

As when a younger-sister-haunted older
daughter finds in the messy street debris
stretch marks on the trunk of an aspen,
etchings of beetles on the tree bark:
or when I photographed the births of my three
children, each in their turn, I saw
that with their first intake of breath
their whole bodies were suffused
with off-hour rainbowing, from head to toe.

Research into Haloes

I don't make good use of winter days
for the needy dead, their hands as I had
arranged them.

Why did he call himself Stone, or House,
or Garment, or Cluster of Henna?
He possessed the will without a why,
before the soul was made a lady by it.

In the meantime (and it is always
in the meantime) your guess is as good as mine,
whether you will hear from your daughter
when she is in her grave

with an ear grown tender to such pleasing minstrels
as that first swallow through the little
Jesus window.

I had to search for a safe place
on the red-hot rim
after two brightly lighted trains
passed one after the other:

I have sent you the betrothal gifts —
a duchesse pear, clocked stockings,
a skirt made from soldier's cloth
by my Farnearness.

In prayer she floats to the tops of trees,
or spires, she stabs her hand with paperclips,
her breasts give forth an oil from which
she is able to feed herself
when arrested, outside the town.

Woman Examining Her Breasts in a Mirror

Why do I always return to the sunken road
through corroded hills where the moon entered
the double-shuttered windows? Who would forbid
light being taken from neighbouring light?

Keep far away, you slender headboards
and you long borders who cover half the feet.
He is reading with his right finger a stretched breast
the new muse has unwoven.

Overflow of flowers in the wilder bit of the garden.
He teaches by what juices kisses disappear
from the holy land of the body
where swallows now are seldom seen singly.

Around the foreshore a straggling absence
of banners trembling on church steeples:
the sea is splashed by stars and rented
nailspaces along alleyways.

The war-scalloped square is attacked
by brightness. The rain-gathering
uplands breathe uninterrupted
views of Government House.

The Nth of Marchember

The way she was standing told me
it wasn't worth going to the trouble
of turning on any more lights.

She guards her blouse, momentarily
holding her heart as if caressing a character
in someone else's family romance.

Within her inner theatre, and seemingly borderless
surround, she quivers across the porcelain
of evening — the bed is certainly more

than it needed to be. When sleep undresses
her mind to even make peace with the city of 'I will',
her blood forewarns her

she is out, out of town, I understand, thumb
on the doorbell, outside, overflying a snowy
border, angel and puppet coming together

in an Old Believer Cemetery whose miracles
take place around boats and water.
For something, read a large half,

a whole self too much — light of my life,
the lanugo of her own splendid body
hobbling my life with its bloody repast.

Those flayed surfaces of her hand are washed
four or five times a day, till the accent
of our parents is fully purged

through our father's cast-off Royal Underwood.
Her undeadness, her petrified unrest
is the ending of time within her,

the alleged redemption's
copy of a grievous gift, flinging her
in and out of the downtown.

The Museum of Touch

Living double one's time
is like swimming across the moon.
She began her song of
'All things have but a time',
before I got the birds drawn.

The double-wicked candles
rippled on a regal swag
of curtain, new birds
would hover round, white
sparrows, a pet whitethroat.

Waterloo is the genteelest
colour, sleeves are now
worn to the elbow with long
gloves for walking dress,
the necks as low as ever
and the bonnets small.

I purchased today a brown
silk umbrella, a noteworthy
Christ, a much reworked
crucifix and a Noli Me Tangere
canvas for a better time.

Cousin Alice

Your mountain is robed in sombre rifle green
and one of its greener fields is suddenly
black with rooks. The stream too seems
to be gone out of town, the lamp sulky
in the dead zone around the river's mouth.

Rainwater captures a much more drive-by
world; we pretend to acknowledge
that we fall short of its perfection,
noting the delicate colouring of the lark,
her half-shadowed ear and turned neck.

It is curious how it is done at once,
your eyes are darkened wholly to dry
up the green from the field. The dozing
cupids on the clock lean a little back-
wards, making a shrine of your bed

which flames in the thinnest of threads, is blue fire
that cannot be painted. Nothing more earthly
than you, posing as the southwest wind
steering the flower car, reading the church,
while Paradise moves inside us

its narrow wicket gate and watchful porter.
Your last control of vision was sunprints
of leaves, from two embrowned chestnut trees,
all opened ground for one who has
just finished her first primrose.

A Supplement to the Withering

The evening primrose always is,
and always will be, a memento
of what I will no longer enjoy on earth.

The snowdrop of 1786 is not green,
nor is it white, nor gold, nor purple,
but an union or offspring of all these.

Our not-the-daughter, not-the-wife,
wore a headdress named the kitchen garden
with vegetables attached to her sidecurls,

and her gown was a closely detailed
landscape scene, the bottom of her petticoat
had brown hills covered with all sorts

of weeds, many of their leaves finished
with gold. Every breadth had an old stump
of a tree, that ran up almost to the top,

broken and ragged and worked
with brown chenille. Her robings
and facings were little green banks,

her sleeves loose twining branches:
we must build a statue of a lioness with no
tongue, but a bag of poems, to honour her.

Corner of Field with Farm

The earth has done its time.
To think that she is dead, she who read
Lamartine in a dark-blue net dress
by the dimlit window, and laughed
so overflowing with a ladle full of holes.

Because I continued to live
during these two months brown-toned boats
look appealing in partial sun.
I discovered a photograph
of my beautiful sculpted daughter
at twelve, in an old box.

I had tortured myself to resemble what I thought
she desired me to be, stretched like wet gloves
worn thin by a long journey. Between her
and me, from the other to me,
no word, no hand, shut doors.

She airs her grievances to Papa, even closer
under the umbrella. It was as if he had shaken
my hand very hard. The beauty of an image
born of us is simultaneously
the most self and the most the other.
She is nothing to me.

She is full of inner happenings,
the house does the rest with its full smell.
Her black collar folds like the waves
in her hair, her white twilights
grow tepid underneath my head.

Broken Pot Used as Writing Material

Re-entry to your eco-niche
is like the beautifying of a cathedral.
One reads these cloths of stem stitch,
laid or couched stitch as natural numbers,
one reads a clock from 12 to 6
asserting that they moved when they didn't.

Boundaries shift for the whole hand,
the left must close a pattern guided
by the right, since signals from the two eyes
fail to recognize an everyday face.

Every third word is a repetitive
covering of the mouth: you swim
from core state to fugue state
in undirected milky water
to a black-filled circle,
which is your fully fledged city
dwindled into a village.

Woman Kept in a Casket

Were it graven with needle gravers on the eye corners
it would be a warning told by women to other women,
an inner story, an evening fable, after the sunset prayer,
in the beaten high road, when the Nile puts on its coat
of mail and shield.
                    Beginning with our commonplace,
'Whatever you do, do not open that door', but he will
certainly open it . . . In a perfectly round city
made of brass, the vizier's daughter, Rose-in-Hood,
paces out the earth around the wax candle market,
wearing red leather trousers, Aleppo jasmine,
and a little dagger. She eats figs and pomegranates,
Hebron peaches, Syrian cheese and, posing as an apparition
of Jesus, she coughs to attract the most affable archangel
of the Brethren of Purity.
                    Her mosquito net of crimson weed
is fastened with flaps of pearl as big as hazel nuts.
Her finger in her mouth means he is like her own body's
soul to her: she bites her hand in repentance, holds the left
against the right in regret. When she strikes upon her breast
with her palm outstretched it means Ahmad the Sickness,
the five divisions of this seed, he should come back
in five days.
                  She must be clumsy when rising and lose
her breath when moving quickly, like a tortoise with a lighted
candle on its back — she must be so stout as to nearly
fall asleep, her sloping hips so fleshly as to impede her passage
through a door, her hind cheeks like mounds of sand
or bolsters stuffed with ostrich down. The quicksilver
of her eyesocket must not be haggard with camel ticks
or gum arabic, or none nighteth there, with a poisoned
book that is rotten inside.
                  For under the roots of the sea,
and the innumerable sounds of footsteps tormenting
the surface of the globe, there is a mirror made

from human eyes by the evil of sorceresses who blow on knots
in their quest for the teeth or vertebrae of the story's
selfish wordstring.

Kaluza's Law

The lake, with its almost healed scar,
in its blue-grey withdrawal is all arms,
badge of white on the thigh. A foggy day
turns white linen brown and faintly browns
the meagre winter flowers, displaying
this degree of wear and tear, a quality of decay
in the sky.

A half imaginary Irish saint
is stepping after the sibyl in praise of moss
and its unvarying thin green notebooks
where the letters of her heather coiffure are lost
through eye-skip. Spry enough,
the blackish flowers in their bowlful of time,
with its inlay of lakes.

An older angel protrudes from the blue
shadow of a church, from pew ends with poppies,
caretaker of seven sparsely feathered wings.
The arrowshaft hastens with its feather gear,
the flukes on the arrowhead bend the sedge
double out on the heath.

Then the slow chamfering of a stone's edge
by blown sandgrains, while the still-fluttering
goatmoth settles for stillness.

Maroon-backed Ledger

When to be how, to change to aqua dress,
asking me down. Her eighteenth summer.
Leaf-arched streets and dewdrops repeating
lay, Sylvie, lay.

His voice tightens the tract, wing-thin and numbed.
My name cutting pleasantly into my cheek,
wearing a thick kelly-green coat
always in the house like a caul.

Tired in brown, I thought about the shock treatment
last night, the breakfast not coming,
crossing the slippery floor between steel cars
coming from all angles, a dowdy stonedrop.

The old dark surface of the photo taken
sixty years ago skipped a week.
My handwriting gone all wild and wracked
neatened for nothing.

The sun set on time like polished barbed wire.
I clocked it, my hand a frost-moth
between my breasts, as though an angel had hauled me
by the hair in a shiver of gooseflesh.

Now, with a sense of in, I see a weather, new ivy,
fog blowing by the geography of certain hills.
The island looks closer with the sea that bathes Sicily
behind it, and won't overlap with other women.

Her Everyday Comportment

There were days a few weeks ago when she was impossible
to reach: today she is findable. Although she is transparent
she looks too Juliet.

What roads are open to her, crouching deeply,
gradually repositioning, suddenly motioning with white
knuckles to sky or earth? She appears to be
not watching, her back flexed to the street
which was my religion.

No amount of suspicion was too much,
knotted into the shift from one half-year
to the other, as if God were in a sense
changing nest, tilted over in that humid shadow,
snowy hands soft as grapes.

She learns to lean leadenly, career as if drunk,
her ear guiding her rotating head whose cramped
neck swivels and makes it swim
as if she is using her head as a limb.

She learns to fall well from her despised waist,
refusing to be stationary, her late-deafened
widowed voice tuning her disconnected speech.
She takes a Saint Christopher medal from her necklace
into her mouth, kissing the tip of her thumb.

A mourning cross between my eyebrows
returns to those gestures and freezes that last
close-up of her lips, as night lies flat on her
and rain grows on the sea . . .

The Seven Times Mother

Her once silver heart ceaselessly keeps watch
like a plucking hand removing dust
from a hidden image. She wears at-home clothing
in her hyper-ornamented space,
her inner muslin's dot and line
rhyming with the curtains directly across
the lively iron table.

Flameless candles pale
the still warm wood colour of her hair
whose sudden turbulence paints
blazing hearths among the leaves:

no little beauty, this preparatory hue,
as when you learn that someone has died
while facing your lips in a mirror,
or soldiers trying to dream
of a good wound.

She Wears the Sky

The horizon line embraces the drowsy river docks:
the deep peacock patch of water reaching the dark
blends with it.

The hills pick up a saintly pallor
from the skin of one doing penitence.
The swallows linger, as if they forgot.

I gaze into the sealed eyes of my mother,
seen, not visited, not forgotten,
in the centre of her own picture,
who wove her own background
with no Martha-work to be done,
as women look when they return to their places
errorless after Communion.

In her rare low moods
she remembers the next five days as twelve
and compares an unheard-of number of things
to be abreast of the incurable,
having no choice but to return
to the end of thought.

In the evenings I can switch the light on from indoors
to illuminate the shroud
of irises over the urn of jasmine.

Goddess of the Candlelight during Childbirth

The weekday gods have blocked the windows with thorns.
We breathe nothing but working-class blue, fires of male
olive, the heavy grace of deeper yellow roses.

Star risings and settings are such dangerous angels.
The tangible hand at the centre of things
is a large red J
rounded up to eat grass in the town square.

Lines of darkness put around the heel of her hand
on its cursive grey surroundings
shiver into strong silver — it barely does its work
of holding the cashmere shawl.

The stab of her thumb back towards her body
is doll-like. Silence issues from her
as from a drowned or empty ship,
or the damp of a single low word.

Not that I dream of describing her near shoulder,
in one of her states, her presence simple
as absence, her face's disturbing perfume,
how she is a scent, the faded bead of her nipple.

The Mirroring Mother

Places resemble their mother
and I *do* visit, the middle of the tint,
core of spring-summer, the centrepiece
which has not been removed.

With wishes and crosses and shawls
we cover her, leaving a chair
to worry a window, one filtering voice
searching the sea for a beloved isle.

She doesn't pray at all loudly,
nor is it a matter of kneeling
in the shallow here and now,
only the dimmest ghost of a bed

surmounted by a tired brown face,
a gaze more kindly than famished.
Her eyes' deep blindness bleached out
in her chalky skin is crushed against

this wall of light to a single shine
on the water, where north and south
nestle close and low. It may be
the lavender spot on the auburn hair

of a painter's girl, the Alice blue
of her petal tea, her lilac kerchief,
the chaste blue of some lonesome flowers.
There is no more safe light

for the separation, if the seated one
rises, another thing I'm unsure
about, like the part of my name
I will be keeping to protect it.

We use the tune every day,
a sound as of a Burmese gong
through the steady, slow-drip sadness,
the day the there was everywhere,

as if another voice we cannot hear
were answering her whole body's
love for a mirror, or its worth;
as if I were still the same.

Why I Don't Get Down and Pray in the Sunroom

Rain has been pouring on the slave garden, not
the winter storm, beautiful as it was, as though the new
year began with the moon's southing, on January
1st. I can give no very laudable account of my time,
except I dined with Mr Paradise and dear Mrs Careless.

The scarlet-armed chairs with their low-spreading feet
were like the old 'His' and 'Her' altars. I have just bespoke
a flannel dress. She is not worth more than her victuals,
her body halved, its back turned in a goodbye to itself,
her face placed on an orange curve that might have been

a bowl or a gentle hill. It might be my mind making up
the voice, her mind was seriously out, she has yet
to utter a sound. But I knew she thought she meant
what she said, we had simply hit an old confessional wall
in the old coarse gospel, waiting for God to pass from

this conversation, or the return earthward of her eyes
that stared so protractedly at such a cloud from so brief
an Earth. My eyes stayed with the cloud, which was a rain-
bow in itself, four times as broad as the moon then was.
For every line in her forehead I counted the church

bells, the skies choked with stars which was the light
that she'd been hearing. I undid the spell of her fast
prayers, that a matching star, sungrazing, would drop
into the sun its deep and massy stone, as some birds
carry their ghost down to us.

On Cutting One's Finger While Reaching for Jasmine

She talked about the aboutness of life, the eternal
false illumination of the leftover nights, her lavender-
skirted self who paced around the tousled
bedroom, the otherwise good you.

She incessantly made 0s, 0s of all sizes,
0s inside one another, always drawn backwards
in lilac ink by her beckoning finger,
on fine paper, gilded and musked.

Ramrod straight in her harp-backed
horse-grey chair, she beheld the most beauteous
scrawl of the same love as never
floated to the house as if rainwater

captured in the water-whipped square
from thundering icequakes and the smaller
curves of a river missing its valley
were the one place a flying creature could feel safe.

Willowware Cup

She can no longer pretend to be
looking through an open window
at sea ringing the city, through
the skypaint which appears
to have been brushed around the house.

Still I judge her life still saved
though I say it who shouldn't,
give or take a few months,
this connection between the two winters,
a love that can exist only in summer.

How can the thought of her
take her away, grain by coral grain,
beyond the reach of outstretched arms
as though the reflection of her here,
and then there, were lying in a grape,

whirl of rose and lemon? All at once
four colours have settled on her
as impermanently as snowflakes brushing
the tree at the gate, their haloes
like ointment or dough, yellow-white

translucence along her underbreast's
new nipple, harsher silver wrist
movements pushing her left side
gently back without smothering
what might be (please let it be!)

her hand, which also never turned
to the back of the book but Mary-like,
clearly suffered decades long
in the idealized garden.
The mere gathers in the curtains

make her sit up in a false glare
though cheek touches floor,
and the knuckles of her skirt's
plain-weave linen, unaltered
at the hem, are yours

more than ever, the careful flesh
of her formless back as it is known to be
by the no longer existing ceiling,
of her rained-in pupil; by the autumn
rustling to pieces the roadside elm.

Sweet Dream Just Before Christmas

One night she thinks she sleeps, the next not.
She has the God-virus, outside the non-God box,
which shades off into the instant like a special train
not in the timetable.
                    The earth is on the move
like broken ice: decorations, processions, rain
over the graves when the shooting ended, before
new shooting began. The city is splashed
by the yelp of one's bell.
                    Her characteristics,
two or three fathoms, she does not speak. To ease her
tongue — to ease my tongue — I look through airs, waters,
places, for old serf-work, in a burnt notebook for
a lightword, childword, wordflesh of his beautyglory,
yes, we know, we know, or his glorybeauty.

Sandpaper Letters

The post-war driftwood is stored away
in drawers of silence, bled into the rug,
whatever the wave might suppose.

In order to remain in love,
to see the city reshape itself
in the dangerless September,
the last page is written upside down.

Galaxies dissipate, while the new spring
learns tranquil abiding, recent birth
of leaves and breeding of grass
as if painting your hand with warmth,
at least for the sake of spring.

Her eyes gone hyacinth in colour,
she is now able to see an entire garden
instead of bits and pieces of plants,
but fixes her attention for hours
on the whorls of her fingers,
being wistful about being human.

She is afraid of a small piece of chain
that looks out of place in a room
pulsating off and on — trying to keep
everything the same: yellow ladder
against grey wall, silver atoms
on a platinum surface, green
slippers with flowers on them.

She would speak only when certain
music was played: with small auditory
tune-outs in the partly heard song
she starts to daydream, as if she were tuned
to a vacant television channel.

I sometimes hear her total bewilderment
about other people's unbalanced minds
injected suddenly without warning,

the faint pure tones
of her heartbeat in my ears.

The Meaning of Margaret's Hands

You — are you? — isn't it all the same?
Her lived space is a match burning in a crocus.
Sunk flatly in on the landing, she slumps
listless, saddened, patient as cattle,
and concentrates on holding her smile in place.

She might be looking down, not across,
the way a curtain hangs and stirs
beyond a surging diagonal of long-necked flowers,
their breasts sky-blue.
Her slightly poisonous, wasp-yellow cushion intrudes
so her slope-shouldered shadow has leaked out
in a strand of amber.

She seems eaten away by the air that surrounds her,
draws her fluid shawl about her to one side
like a sainted, earthen person.
A bracelet that tastes salty repeatedly falls down
on her wrist, where her finger and thumb
serve as sugar-tongs with muted purple
underlights in her fingernails.

She is twisted forward down into herself,
the weight of her torso supported like a wheelbarrow.
Her breasts, that let themselves be searched for,
shift and swing in the enormous dress
with its puffs and bell-skirts.
She carries them like a purse in which
the outline of her ribs screens any gaze
upon them, she rests them through the peach
of her heart on a dilapidated pillow.

When the day-bell sounds or the wine-bell
shuts the taverns, her chair becomes a lap
for the tissue tension of her heavy thighs.

She lays her face on the water of a vase
located around her head. A switch
of acid colour within her cut-open eye
grazes the alert forcelines of her hair,

as her hands are taken from her, handed over
like the lightest foot of a footed bowl
to which we give the name 'Care' and unpack it.

Something as mobile as a human being
gives that roundabout kiss to the keepsake
of her lungs where every window
shuddered the withoutness of the obliterated hotel
while children were being born.

Seated Woman

Her cheek clenched like a leather butterfly,
she remains hard to love, heartless sometimes
as fruit painted sullen red on coffee cups, as mallows
fossilized in silver wire against the gold couch.

All but speechless, she is mildly grazing the dry
re-wilded air, the clouds' salinity,
her face in sliding light skimmed
from the inexhaustible street like rain-fed rice.

Her taupe dress is too flat to be a room,
too brown to be outdoors, but hyperlucid
as the windfield that rubs shoulders with you,
as if you were running your hands through a climate.

The Mercyseat

Though Sunday my mother begins it.
Her fingers strike each other like wood,
moth-sand to her ear above
in the skymole light. For a year
she has eaten nothing but ginger.

There are large, tear-shaped areas
in her eye viewed from side-on,
however mousy, fin shapes and a trumpet-
void, as though she were living
without a heart, her merest yearning edge.

And sometimes she revolves in bed
like a roast before a fire.
Her Citherean temple is a nest-scene
on a birdlip mirror, a byway
of tenderness, as when arms seem

flung out from a centre.
I have a sort of cobweb feeling
that we understand how much she wants
to be understood, hearing
the grass grow and the squirrel's heart beat.

The Spirit of the Mother

How too far, as early as late,
the notch of blue sky shadows her breasts with blue,
her blouse pinned by a ruby, her proud and pleatless
dress, the low table bearing common fruit.

No round of body is thinkable
this side of the silhouette,
hunched, sightless figure,
bedded-down, full-blown brooder.

Her elbows are lifted, peaked elbow,
soaring elbow, till her hoisted elbows
swathe her head, discharged
from a difficult crouch.

With fossil curtains beyond and behind
in a setting of petrified plush,
she is drowsing, dying,
in her ill-timed sleep,

a primitive crust,
heaving and folding,
encapsulated
in her own spatial pale.

Those sealed lids, which can never yet
have been open, startled,
fix the visitant with their ravening stare,
and tighten their lock,

close-knit, close-valued,
on her constant slant
from ground to sky
no longer possessable.

She resonates in every corner,
woman half-length, upright, asleep,
a deeper hold
to wrench away from.

Her body bulks from the lower right
up to the levelled forearm,
the plane of her chest props
the tipping beam of her collarbone

whose incline edges the neck
overlapping the crest of her shoulder.
All this weight of a woman
hangs on the jostling behaviour
of tangent colours, their hithering-thithering
functions.

Directed air circulates
her visible margins and averted sides,
sternum and spine outflanking her
to upstage one another
by dint of wayward shadows
in a continuously looped surface.

The tabled glass is at hand,
the remoter, spearhead pear
cleaves to the goblet, to that opaque
backdrop of sky that lies beyond access,
a firmament laid piecemeal with shingles
releasing the collusive parqueting
on her in-face.

An incontinent door seeps
into the pathway from home,
into outdoors, luminous perforations

where we expect solid core.
The square door encourages breathing,
sweeps of sortie instead of a barren threshold,
converts the glissading flesh
of her incomplete, terminal members
to the mild elevation of a living being.

Her figure seems pressed on all sides,
the strap of her neck drops to her chest,
the knot of its shoulder wanting its proper span,
the throw from cheekbone to ear slow-rolling,
slightly ruffled, her wattled eye
adrift from the given carnations.

You'd think her mouth was a thing worn out
like a brooch or badge by brutal outpouring,
its gnawed-at curve a thicket
too sudden-bright to be satisfied.

What exactly compounds
her invertible summit? Few streets
have been so pierced: the shadows appear
to be those of midday, and her subjacent phantom,
the hospitality to such shadow,
a mummy-brown, pocket-edged in black.

The High Caul Cap

The October rains set an all-time record:
all arrivals and departures were in doubt;
the airlines were on strike, it seems, in honour
of the water; in raining mountains, bad, sweet smells.

Calm spiders in the morning rivers,
gusts of birds, melody of bells.
When the heavens duly open
dead leaves explode underfoot.

This cold rain, from a cloud that had
unaccountably overslept, overtakes us
every afternoon like a vague
melancholy from some other autumn.

An immense red blossom, whose name
stops just in time, is the last candidate
for light; she pulls herself along like a broken
cricket, past the lifeless houses.

Sunburst in E Major

The gods at this time of the year
are partly about praying. All the sadder
she is blind-eyed in the midst
of this enormous web she has spun.

A tragedy as of dumbness itself,
as if speaking hurt her passive fortress,
never safe to be seen in pieces,
she no longer needs this helper's calm

to order her to have the dream.
Turning mist and whistling wind
have skimmed her house to the bone
and, as for rain, magenta rainclouds

embroider the ocean-garden with tinted
leaves not clinging to their blooming.
The white-browed robin hops heavily
on crutch-like branches, white and mossy

as a bridal veil over the simplified river —
the white-naped honeyeater flies away
in the shape of a cross to the clear sedation
of the re-meandered street.

Far from having to be recalled to mind,
my love is in a walkable attire,
like an angel wearing lipstick,
heart not so heavy as mine.

The Vine Forestlight

Placing her thumb at the first joint
of her index finger, she pretends to free
her dress studded with ears of corn
from branches where it is not caught.

Leaf-birds at the cruder, cut-out windows
lay their silk invasion map
on the table's dove-shaped ciborium:
soon her face will wake its drynesses

in the open alley of a goodly garden.
She has been given a rose for a heart,
its last layer of red the measure
of that pennyroyal of yours,

and with that monstrous flower holds
a rainbow bodily in her hand
like a lotus-fibre bracelet.
Time and sunlight circulate,

well-spent, but when discalced night gushes
forth into the prim gold of those perfect,
steady irises, the scar will be
like the Croix de Lorraine

on that lace surcoat knit of pearls
which is the meaning of the room,
the moth-balled, jewelled glove
I wear on my shoe.

Rose Inhabited by a Bee

Candlemas. The town neither lighted nor watched.
Daylight increasing by three minutes, except for her
a blue less bright, a pink less intense.

With one long stroke the young man,
with upturned knife, his *nota bene* hand
in its sleeve, cuff or glove, has channelled
between two pages so that her red and deep lavender
stylized cloud will soon be replaced.

For now she remains a letter halved
between rose and radiance, a pseudo-flower
with angel-supporters in gold gowns
white-shading her unspoken outline:

the colours abnormally darkened just-off
straight, leaves filling her spine-fretted space
with dampened green dots and grey button loops
that render her, more or less, alone.

Master of the Female Half-lengths

Mother and daughter, you orbit them both
in their tight widowhood. Her bleak indispositions
whistled up my veins as though they were vacating
houses into which we never moved.

She drank vodka out of a salt cellar
under a melon pavilion, or bean shed,
in a grape garden, till the loosened clang
of round-the-clock daylight

prolonged her endurance of drowning.
Eggwhite bursting seas depearled
the ship not made of flesh, began
to remove its more delicate sails

while broom stars fell apart gently.
I went about my stilling, dressed
the chamber, set up the green velvet bed,
and made an end of my Irish-stitch cushion.

I came to keep my fish days,
sent cordials and conserves, a salt-powder
to put in her beer, since her throat
quakes from time to time

as dark tendrils of her brain snowbud
the growth of that violet sunset.

The Doll Funeral

Those who live inside the year,
in its ever greater lateness,
are uncertain of its ability to end
when the calendar turns over.

It is more like the weakness
of my mind than the strength of yours,
as if there were no such serpent
in the slice of the house, in the wide town.

During the next month she came round
to a perusal of her bracelets
and her ultra-Irish body, the marriage
that might be in the north of the future air.

My two-piece calico, clockwork, creeping
doll, so indestructible, so heavy she was
moved about on rollers
with large, protruding gears,

my talking doll nearly as perfect
as machinery could be, enigmatic,
vain, mute and delicate, with voice
too faint to be heard,

when the sheet music inside
her doll head, with two opposite faces
and movable lower lip, stuck,
buzzing like an entrapped bee.

A Death Horoscope

On one side rises a limestone wall.
The wall and the curve never seem to end
but then, as they do, as the road digresses
from the wall, the pull of the bend
is still with you and the wall is yours.

Beyond her eyelids the famous fountain
flames with wine in October, rousing whole
mountains, one called Bloody. Dark leaves peak
to an impossible staircase of supersaturated red
in a tower of silence made from lambswool.

Eden's courtesy drags blossoms on her muscles
like the weight of contrition on the smallness
of her soul. The splendour of decay moments
begins the innermost failing of ghostly health,
weaving the perfumed voices through her voice.

Dormition: Madonna with Trees

I suppose today is more or less your birthday:
I pray you, send one word
whether I shall maintain your taper in the chapel.

Our mother, who never seemed to sit down,
takes nothing but broth;
she has crazed eyes, her singing voice out of tune

in any case — how did this one find
her speaking voice? She leaves her next thought
unknown, the unshared thoughts

fall through her upper arms
and through my left arm runs
a flood of striped silk.

The next breathing movement
is a halt in breathing: the throttling sentence
pulls itself together and stops

on the threshold of a rimy minerality.
She does not recover
an ordinary life, tightens like stone

or ebony, cracks, bleeds, decays,
splits into at least four of us,
almost not to move and not to end

but only to dissolve
in an elsewhere that racks her.
I am a slow listener,

should anything be too outstretched
for her hands. I had myself wheeled
into that peaceful room many a time.

She is full of clouds, broken, refashioned,
and infinite, her far side shot through
with blue ovals, moulding thus

a cape towards white,
reminding us there are limits
to how long we can follow her.

In the width of the untrimmed window
the sea lies very quiet with a last
essential light in it

where the house shuts up narrow.
We fear her not to be
of our world at all, her winged breasts

pleated and yellow:
time to ripen up to him.
I turn my microphone then

a little over the yew trees,
the willows old as from the middle ages,
all forming a sort of chalice.

She liked to have a line
around her — the line seems guided
by a sweet jubilation where she is not.

It is she who appears
ready to leave — we mainly lose
a music, or a boat sunk

containing her as music.
All of this, her searching odyssey,
her disintegrating voyage,

must be slipped into silk herbs
by the tips of fingers only.
Now all of the bodies

stand to one edge of the drapery,
without releasing, go beyond her,
so that she may stall and anchor there.

Gold Star Mother

for Carole

The fields are loosened
by the most complete spring,
the most everlasting, most glistening,

when the super-essential light
always seems to win, yet your plumage
was poor, sorrow-creating, reddish spring.

She asks to be touched on her body white
just like the snow at Christmas,
her selfhood a cloak with drops of smithied
silver over her shoulders.

Water applied to her head evaporates
like a sponge on an oven: her almost polar
eye streams blood.

She audibly does not say several things
that occur to her, mouth joining and parting
like an immature flower.

I hear her heart pound as she emits
every fibre of her being,
her arm aching with the force.

We listen to a new kind of silence,
her semiconscious, unconscious
out-of-syncness I have never seen before.

Gnawing waves hidden
in her wispy branches bare
a stone doorway, scarred and shorn,

a charred door handle, to what
there might be, over there:
something that comes from the hills,
something like a countenance,
as the sawn-through tree is skyborne.

The Plumrose Anemone

The lime coral alters and recrystallizes, slipping
between things. In the afternoon yellow
a breast-sling is paired by its shadow.

Purple wreathwort twists its old leaf
in her ovary, or a leaf about to be old,
gifted with a flower. She keeps to the corners
of her counterpane, her bed covered
with plates and dishes. Her veins are parallel
like pillars of books, her skirt is stretched out
at the hips where her canvas petticoat
gapes open. She wears a foul mob
over the perfect, glossy folds of her hair,
thus gambling with her grace.

At the wind-rounded hour of low water
we drape her with bright red fabric
most gratefully fragrant. The currach
sleeps on its back in the grass,
the curve of its belly upturned like a star
washed ashore by the abolition of all metaphor.

Operation Spring Wind

Rome did not die in a battle — Rome's death
lasted centuries. Where is that mournful sadness
located, when you come closer? Do you see her
eyes and mouth there? Look away, and they
have vanished; it's just a hand stirring
flashes of great beauty.

A gold strap for all the sleeve thought necessary,
the mask she wears will stay for the rest of her life.
What a pleasure not to have any strength and not
to need any — weakened by books and fearing
the light of day. We must first clear
the air that surrounds her,

a splintered country that has lost its soul,
somewhere between decay and the piercing
smell of flowers whose edges are made
of wind and rain. It is not the rainbow
that polishes the dust from the mirror
of the moon. Don't suppose it is the new moon

whose flavour remains in the thirsty mind,
in the moist neck, that brings such sweetness
to the throat. The disc of the sun wanders distracted,
like an atom, world-warming, world-seeing,
morning out of love. No woman covers her breast.
Yesterday your fortunate sister was here.

Let's look at the water of life flowing out
of the dragon, those plump corporeal tulips in the fountain-
spout of moonlight. The angels so thronged together
to watch you, mother-of-pearl body white as cotton.
You with the crescent brows and interwoven ink motif —
don't suppose it is the current that halts the boat here.

The Honey Vision

Her left hand that was agile with temporal intervals
limpingly withdraws, ever weaker, now untouchable.
Her life-breath forms a honeycomb in her mouth
as if breathing in but never out. I hear her breathless
breast panting, though no distance makes her weary.

There it would be, a sunbeam settling so fiercely
on her face it could only have come from within.
Her children absorb into her, she dissolves into herself,
unwintry as the very look of spring coming
intentionally lost along the wooded road.

I thought even the dust could crush her bird dress
in walnut and rosewood case, to turn to silver
for nineteen years under the tree. We are not
to think of it as opulence, or a credence of summer;
the kingdom of heaven has to be seized by force.

She may on her return return, in other jet-black
moments beyond the need for any unction.
Now stolen away from the eyes' pursuit she remains
an open eye, the rose with homeward ripening
wilts somewhere in the middle of a field.

Ascent to Perception Temple

Black pourings from the heavenly blackboards,
lukewarm sun darkening so quickly, a trembling,
radiant maroon. There is a welcome at the door
to which no one comes, a clumsy body holding back
an airy spirit, withered by the intense gleam.

Floor-bound, inward-looking, with her voice of beaten
tin and scorched throat, she seems to be shuddering
herself to pieces in the mid-reaches of eternity.
Nightingale without eyes, bird in orbit, she retains
her hands, her wing still partly an arm, gazes
at what is still left of her breasts.

The remembered children are keenly solaced,
though this heaven has collapsed forever,
by this winged calling of tragic angels
who do not themselves suffer,
her scrupulous gladdening a moment in some
past May, ending suddenly against his heart.

The Wearing of Brooches

Beautiful God on the dirtfloor,
his black is more precious than most people's crimson.
In this autumn of all others
too little remains of its mottled bark colour,
the terminal leaf grows out of a kind of urn,
a kind of punctuation.

I am in lavender on a lightweight shelf
all day, reading downhill
the seamless endurance exactly as it leaves your lips,
as though around the gemmed edge
of this jewel, the whole purse-lid
surface of the buckle,

laid on a bed of interlace
in the carpet-page, in a crouching pose
and lack of fore-leg, book shrine,
bell shrine, nestling within the arms of an earthfast
cross, its tips ending in hooks,
ensnared in a deer trap.

A seated harpist, with scar of a body,
prism head and veiled hands tucked amongst garments,
pear-shaped hip to shoulder, trunk
so slender, covered under the footcone
and the bowl-girdle, spiralled joints
sitting slightly proud of the flexed knee.

There is no real over or under
to the beaded elbow or looped bend
of the surviving arm. In one preserved
corner of the kite-brooch
four white stitches float around a dark
granule at the back of the mouth.

It is their very nature to be twisted,
though the glass eyes, cast in a silver economy,
the detailed pupils,
the decorated breast, give a sure dawn feeling
that the bird has flown free of any frame.

The Mules that Angels Ride

Some islands have two springs and two autumns;
she, whose favourite word is or, not thus,
has like a blindness scoured taken the name
of this island as her deep abiding surname.

In a semblance of an atmosphere
there is birdlife and therefore birdsong
to sweeten her three ear-bones and her four-
chambered heart. She faces left again

towards the mere outwardness of air, gas
scented to smell like appleblossoms.
No steps of grey between the blue star
and the gold star, those two mornings.

With their double refraining of her mortified,
almost translucent body, discarded,
outdated, redundant material, whose
inert, sterile time is crowned

by circular capitals of daylight,
massings of the workaday shrubs
the peaceful oneness of day and night:

she has been passed over a wall
that has no opening, by a bloody,
green-winged, red-crowned angel

known to have lost its head
in its long-pondered surrender to total
leaflessness, reached down glistening from a shelf.

The Skull Nest

You, my field of heavy-jowled horses
with heads facing opposite directions, one
pictured inside the other — no grass is ever shown.

We speak of the rain as if it were an animal,
the she-rain, with her nearly sleeping face.

Open or closed, her eyes are all-important,
eyes of cowrie-shell, charcoal-smeared;
their diamond-shaped irises can become any
colour, like the perfectly white piece
of quartz he sings into her forehead.

The ghost of his fingers curls, as if a fishhook
is dragging her scalp. Her body wafts gently
up and down like a scarf in a breeze.
Her two bent arms join hands
in a full-blooded haunting, bisected by a river.

With a gourd over her skull, she is placed
in a canoe cut in half and doubled over,
her eye spirits in the Epiphany frost
simple snow lights, Shakespeare-scented,
beneath living floors.

Dúlamán

No man knows of my impulse,
the vein in my armpit severed
from dry crying.

The yellow blackbird
is troubled by the bell
each stormless winter:

birdfeather and down
on one bed together,
a coffin made of five different trees.

Sung Death

This upright girl in her jar could be a painting
of a white Jesus, though there is never any blood.
How can she stay put, shifting from long to short,
a screen that looks at you like a stone when framed?

Two acrobats form the fungused O of her mouth,
for a mouth can be crowned by another mouth. The black
cap of her hair is plastered down, *à la garçonne*, but is
also the surplice of the angel, her wings its cheeks.

She is never naked; her garment is a promised current
of blue, not filled, a blush which parades. She looks
to the left with her composite heads arching
as if her family of winter were swimming

in a nearby letter, twin yet foe, wrist flourishing
the swarthy red pads of her fingers with their finger
jewels. Movement of serpent through leaves, her eyes
retain the tracery of her first meanings in the coil

of her forehead's overheated tortoiseshell.
Thin clouds pass their blackish robes in front
of the black of her closed eyes, like a single skin.
The mirror bisects and repeats the flower worn

over one ear — its delicate stain. Her eye consists
of a little prune that finally dies to a soft thread
spoken by a good sister. We did not hear her breathe
the admirable vowels, the alighted consonants.

There was no beating except the stunned heart's dreamed-
of stretching; she outskirts the farm towards her own land.

The Ocean River

The tireless sun has already been made to sink,
shrouding itself in fiery bronze beside the moving field
of a reed-bed. The earth has darkened to look like earth
that has been ploughed, although it is gold.

A double stillness which occurs nowhere else
surrounds the metal field ditch, its poles
of silver, fence of tin, a pasturing place
by a river sounding echoes of her personal angel.

A meadow under a cloudy sky stands against
a window open to clouds and a flowery
tree-shade meadow with foaming brambles
where we drank the angel's beauty to our hearts' content.

❖

The shadow of her absence over the perception
of her presence is like light pouring through glass
into beechwood cups. She spends her eyes
like shreds of the mind in neighbouring fields,

blind listener overhearing the conversation
of sighted speakers. Take dolphin's skin,
make it into a whip, bind betony and garlic
in fawn-skin for a very old headache.

When vernal things bother a nightwalker
mix a salve against Lent-illness with lupin,
viper's bugloss, a cloved strawberry-stalk. Never sit,
never sleep, I chant on you a she-wolf's lust and restlessness.

The Light Called Opalesence

Sunlight hammers down through the thin air
but I am waking to the setting sun.
Clouds that haven't passed over land,
unwilling to repeat themselves, ask
what's going to happen to a shredding cloud.

A rope has been stretching, now it breaks.
The river builds its own banks out
of the complicated water. Everything has been said
in her altar of never-to-be-recovered thoughts
studded with buds and shapes of flames and leaves.

I think hard about her using small brooms
for the disconnected dusts of my true weaning.
In dreams of the more recently deceased
I see her with long skirts dancing a clover-leaf
turn into strong wind blowing at the shore.

Notebook of Sleeps

When lust has dragged us from the house
he alone brings the perfumed bread.
When lifelessness leaves the soul,
and sends the sunrise out of us,
the world looks staringly
and we find we need more veil.

I had been feeling the age of the world,
teaching the five-beat line for weeks,
my jetsam images along one keel
being calmed by the ring of blue
and green: Saint Zita for lost keys,
Apollonia for toothache.

Happily, still quick,
my mother departed to God,
her last sleep scented
by the herbage of her breast,
the faint red roof of her mouth
and her grave with its leafy lips.

Sibyl with Guitar

When I look back I don't know
if there have been any nights,
even any difference in light. I don't
hear the city the way I used to

when there was something in me
that could catch fire, like long ago
waiting for a kiss. The moon hides
in the throat of the tone of the yellow

bell. I am willing that the seasons
wear me out. Dead-eyed angel,
lying on her side, white in the daring
dark, her death is the smallest sadness

she was able to cause. A folding
of hands, as if every place knows
about all the others; the patience
of a summer in the rebellion

of her skin; a milky rush
in the curves of a riverbank.

M and a Half Street

I kept a diary of regret,
an unbinding never wholly unbound.
My eyes settled on the lime and black
cover, drying clovebuds when I opened it,
bloom and buzz.

I've still got the clippings about it,
a look given in a handsbreadth
of mirror or these Christmas windows
now and eversame. In a good rain
the vanessa or sphinx moth
could weave me as a ghost
to be near the mother in her dark place —

her imperilled ivory shell,
inner lacy crystals of bone.
And after, after that,
I ran through the next dial down,
whispering when was 52nd Street
still a street.

Buttermilk Shade

The earth beside you
is full of bulbs:
what, if anything, can be done?

Summer and winter meet on the trees.
Something seems gone from the garden
and you cannot tell what.

Large black umbrellas
had been hung from the ceiling
by way of decoration,

beings in the same place
yet not together —
the amusement of the dead

at our wanting to live on,
to buy rainforest, or cloudforest,
and leave it undisturbed

while the warmth from our fields
pours itself unrequited into space
and frightens the flowers blue.

A grey cloud in one piece
plaits dark on the sea
through the crimson pulp of sunset.

Daylight is almost powerless
in the room. For minutes of years
it addresses the fog

on this nocturnal side of speech.
And furniture talks also
in this way:

a taper lighting the stair-rods,
a bulb burning out in the porch
all night;

the vibration of that which is perfect,
the glow at its edges,
is watching the world change.

Dark Lips, Jade Pillow

This end of day the sea arches
spectral waves and a few lingering
souls recall beach-glare
when the sky would have been stronger.

A three-quarter moon of abstract
grey, like a much-needed lung,
as truly alive as any person,
is weighted to the pre-sunset purples.

I take another subtle sky reading,
contrasted with the daybreak sky
some pages back, when clouds aligned,
the come and gone leaf never quite lost.

The Blood Trolley

My mother I did not know at all:
her cameo appearance in the eighteen
frozen mirrors in her room reminded me
of a gold letter on a quartered rose,
of the same pond. Like a heavy mist
at a temperature just above the dewpoint
when its moisture has not yet coalesced
into drops of rain, her heart has moved on,
closèd and unblemished pearl beribboning
the four spokes or rays of the name Jesus.

Beloved document, ash, a residue
on the tongue of the mind, punning red
ink roseshape with deep lines
on her brow's flowing blue, her body
is what has mattered there, registering
in its fluency the steady evaporation
of the person into her stony likeness,
leached away like salts out of a rock.
A bittersweet envoy in black stood
in all this black just waiting to be disrobed.

The name of the mortuary was 'Ultimate Succour'.
Through the tiniest slits I have contrived to make
in the folds of the sari over my eyes
I recognized my mother, selling pickles,
sewing padded armbands, walking through
the Ghetto in a light-coloured coat,
wearing thin shoes with straps, with apples
and pears displayed in a window, waiting
for a coin — she hid her pot in fear when she saw me:
was she fetching milk, was there still milk?

Where was the rickshaw intending to bring
the child with typhoid? Only the better

sort of dead had boxes. The corpse-bearers
wore strange rubber gloves that seemed made
of wood. She was still wearing a blouse,
a beautiful woman of over ninety.
I was led by her through those subterranean
galleries many times, to her haunting world
where already the angels had started
to slam their wings.

Now she seems to be driving
a vehicle with a large skull in front,
or walking a skull on a leash
through marshy riches. I have touched death
with her white bonework, seen dark
things as bright, enchanted by the pleasant
shadow of the rich Christ, saying Peace,
Peace, when there is no peace:
no function for the heart to serve
the dear, the best-known face.

Receiving Non-rebirth

The weakest ring finger, it won't drag the skin.
Her roses sweetened our room: he always chose
a young landscape. It takes twenty years
of journeying to match seen traces with imagined.

Blackened traces of abandoned encampments,
their abode on the hard-packed ground
at the two stony meadows: I stopped there
after twenty years away, at a few black marks

two decades old. The silent traces offered
no guidance to their location, evidence
of people but no people. The vestige of the abode
was hidden from you, though firmly fixed,

until it spoke as if deaf, babbling like a foreigner.
The annual pilgrimage cycles have been completed,
sacred and profane months elapsed. Thundershowers
and spring rain fell on them, plants leafed,

females bore young, her indigo sprinkled in circles.
How do we question rocks forever in one place?
I take their silence for granted,
water running through torrent courses

effaces all but the starkest signs over smooth
stones I cannot read, no artificial lake or gardens.
Assembled folk whose beauty the wind battles,
the wind spends the night baring them,

rolling them away. The eye describes them
as greatly alive, signalling with their hands,
silent. My uncertainty of them grows until
my two hands pursue and touch them:

then they do not recognize my touch. I wonder
if they are transported to that lost time,
an open space beside a tall mountain,
a dream covering the doubt of my eye.

They are clothed in white so that you see of them
but cotton robes. In the wilds a dead deer,
white grass wraps it. But it is the deepest green
possible twice over. I will no longer possess

its hidden virtue and secret, but you will be
luminous, solid memory, petrified moment,
tall guardian of this — but what was it?
Already quarried and reduced to dust.
Already absorbed, already it ferments.
I see myself hereafter in love with the noble
one and all, of every root and source.
Again light shines on the green moss.

The Flower of the Moment of What Comes Easily

She sleeps in respect to herself,
languorous and numbed by the pure
when and where. Her sandal
is without power to mark sound.

She cannot avoid this haunting
to destroy her surface self by as many
resurrections as abandonments,
a swan by day and a young woman by night.

Her image on the window glass jangles
into my room, in the most choked
of voices says nothing to me,
a bandage that the flesh has grown over.

Even the daylight feels as mute
as the fourfold halo of the May moon
or the thoughts we say are ours
when stars lose their nests,

pearl-like letters hidden down
a mineshaft. A storm draws up
that swaying blue sky, its thunders
stolen by plumes of explosions

in pear-shapes like poplars. Thus
the unknown rhythm of her looks
is softly spilled in the youth
of the water, metal-skinned.

When someone refuses to meet
one's eyes, in the long now,
across my face stripes the forever
tangible gaze of my late mother.